I0111282

海豚出版社
DOLPHIN BOOKS
中国国际传播集团

Published in the United States by Flying Tiger Press. Published in China by Dolphin Books.

Original Chinese edition Managed by: Jin Yongbiao and Wu Wei

© 2024 Flying Tiger Press

Flying Tiger Press is the Trademark of Jiang Boyan LLC.

Flying Tiger Press' books are available at special discounts when purchased in bulk for premiums and sales promotions as well as for educational use. For details, please contact us at info@flyingtigerpress.org.

Library of Congress Cataloging-in-Publication Data has been applied for.

Hardcover ISBN: 978-1-963417-11-1
Paperback ISBN: 978-1-963417-21-0
E-book ISBN: 978-1-963417-01-2

Printed in the United States of America
First Edition

The first graphic novel of King Gesar, adapted from the world's longest epic *Gesar*. A Tibetan equivalent of *Odyssey*, the ancient epic remains a living oral literature and has been inscribed in 2009 (4.COM) on UNESCO's Representative List of the Intangible Cultural Heritage of Humanity.

The 10-volume series *The Legend of King Gesar* tells of Gesar's birth, his early years and love stories, and his fight against malevolent forces. Born to be a hero, Gesar has been sent down to the human world to conquer monsters and liberate the people,
but he is framed by his uncle and sent into exile.
Can he finish his mission?

Winner of Best Comic Award of the 5th Asian
Youth Animation & Comics Contest (AYACC)

Winner of Grand Master Prize at the 2nd
Master Cup International Illustration Biennial

Gyanpian Gyamco is a specialist in researching and translating the Tibetan epic *King Gesar* and Tibetan contemporary literature and a doctoral supervisor at the Institute of Ethnic Literature, Chinese Academy of Social Sciences.

Quan Yingsheng is a contemporary artist and member of China Artists Association. He has been making comics, animations, ink paintings and Zen paintings for more than 20 years. His comics and ink paintings have won many awards. He was involved in making 52 episodes of *Journey to the West* produced by China Central Television (CCTV).

Jin Yongbiao is a book and animation planner. He was a journalist, full-time literary translator, editor of a literary magazine, book editor, deputy editor-in-chief and vice president of a publishing house.

Wu Wei is the former Deputy Director of the Third Bureau of China's State Council Information Office and the former Deputy General Manager of China National Publications Import and Export Corporation. Her works include *Biography of King Gesar*.

AN INTRODUCTION TO THE
PRINCIPAL CHARACTERS

Gesar:
the hero of this story; he has come
down to earth to save the world.

Great Master Padmasambhava:
Teacher of Gesar.

Sengcham Cholmo:
the most beautiful girl in the
Ling Tribe and Gesar's queen.

Chona Rinchin:
Gesar's grandfather, the
king of the Dragon Family

Senglong:
Gesar's father,
kindhearted,
gentle and tolerant.

Meto Natse:
Gesar's mother,
the daughter of the
Dragon King.

Chatsa:
Gesar's half brother and a
great hero of the Ling Tribe.

Zhaotoin:
Gesar's uncle, treacherous and
good at using witchcraft.

CONTENTS

Whirr——

No matter what you ask for, we can talk it over.

You are of the same family. If someone should go...

You should go there yourselves!

It is vital for the survival of the Ling Tribe. You don't like my brother?

He is a demon!

I would rather be the prize for the horse race,

than become the slave of that demon!

008

Choro is not a demon!

You were wrong about him that night.

Alas!

As for the horse race...

008

010

In the tent of the chieftain of the Upper Ling

Chalho, if you don't agree, we can get her back.

No, no, it's my family's honor to make a contribution to the Ling Tribe.

I just wonder,

why Cholmo is so willing to go there.

Haw-haw...

Anyhow, it is a good chance for her to toughen up.

Yes!

Ho ho...

Ho ho...

Heck, it's a big world outside.

I should have ridden a horse.

But almost all the yaks and horses were killed by Choro!

I'm going to beg that terrible man! Why didn't my father see me off?

...

Er?

You agree with me, right?

Bow-wow!

Doggie!

Only you are kind to me!

Ta-ta-ta——

Doggie?

What's the matter?

Somebody is coming.

We'd better find a place to hide first.

Pa!

!

Oh?! A person?

Who are you?

Damn. It ran away again!

Hey, put me down!

Whiz——

Just a moment.

Oh? This person...

Oh, no, no. I mean I live in the north. There are lots of bandits here. It will be safe to go with me.

Oh, I see.

Thanks for saving me.

My goodness! This is a trap I set up. I haven't said sorry ...

I meant to catch a horse, not you... Alas!

Gosh!

Doggie? Are you OK?

Ha! Glad you are fine.

Is it yours?

Yes!

I nearly forgot it...

What's your name?

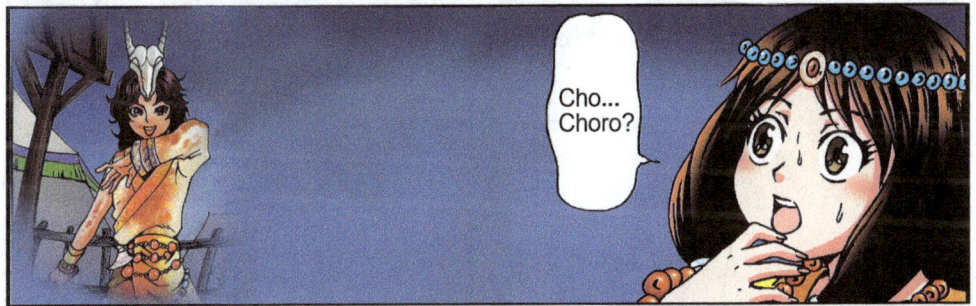

Chapter 7

Gyaingar Pebo

Ta-ta... Ta-ta...

Ta-ta... Ta-ta...

Slow down!

Woof!

Woof!

Hehe!

This horse is quite interesting.

It likes places where tigers and leopards hide themselves.

Whirr! Whirr~~~

The direction should be right.

Woof!

It is my Doggie!

Come back!

Whoosh! Whoosh!

This is...

So many hounds!!

It is Doggie!

Wow! Doggie has finally found its long-lost wild father.

What are they chatting about?

Barking!!

Barking!

How should I know?

Woof!

Woof!

Oh, there it is!

Whirr

Pa!

034

Whiz—

I'm coming!

Pa!

Pa!

Horse, you have finally agreed to carry me!

How beautiful this place is!

043

045

Chapter 8

Heart of the King

Master, are you leaving?

The demons in the north grow more powerful, so I will go and check that.

Well, the Ling Tribe will host horse racing after they move here. Remember to ask Choro to take part in it.

Do you mean the selection of a king by way of winning the horse racing? But Choro shouldn't be interested in it.

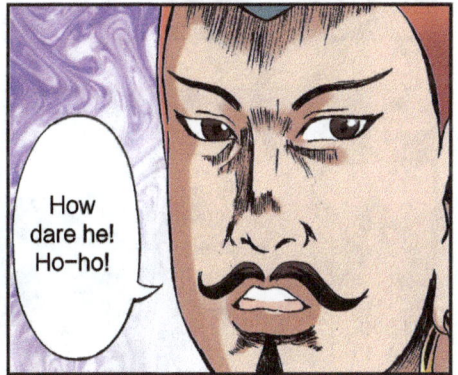

How dare he! Ho-ho!

I...I will persuade him.

047

I thought there was a powerful army here. If I knew it was so easy to move here...

We needn't have begged Choro!

This is not our place. We'd better notify Gormo first.

This is a waste of time!

I will go with you.

OK.

It is really a good place!

I will build my house here at once!

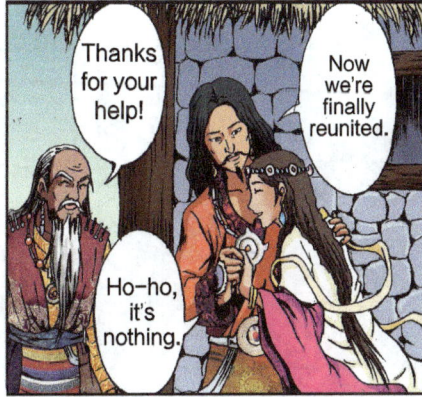

Thanks for your help!

Now we're finally reunited.

Ho–ho, it's nothing.

Mother!

Look who's here!

Gormo!

You've been through a lot.

It was our fault that we didn't keep you.

Let bygones be bygones!

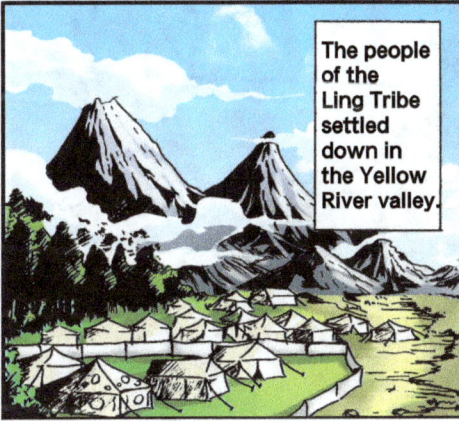

The people of the Ling Tribe settled down in the Yellow River valley.

Several years later, with rich pastures and thriving herds, this place has become their new home.

The horse racing was put on the agenda.

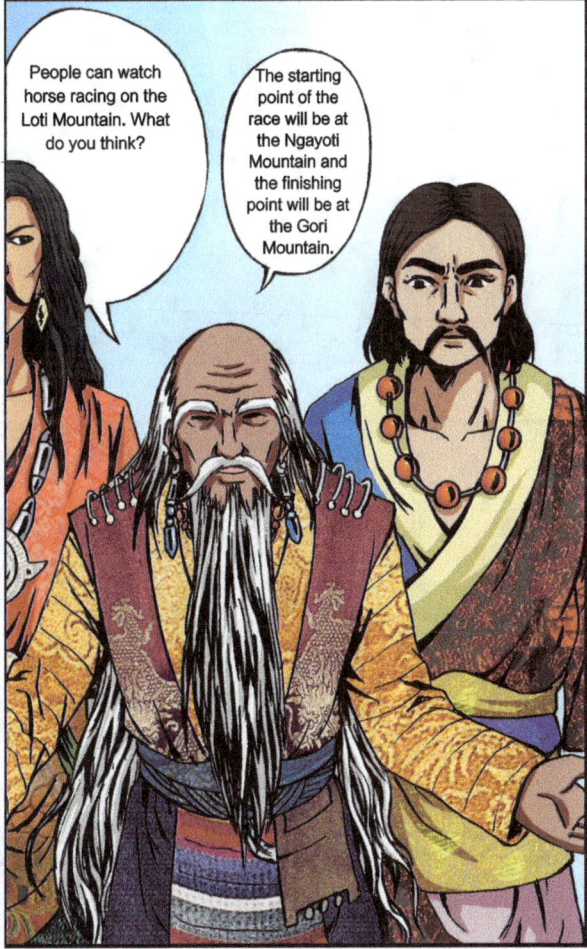

People can watch horse racing on the Loti Mountain. What do you think?

The starting point of the race will be at the Ngayoti Mountain and the finishing point will be at the Gori Mountain.

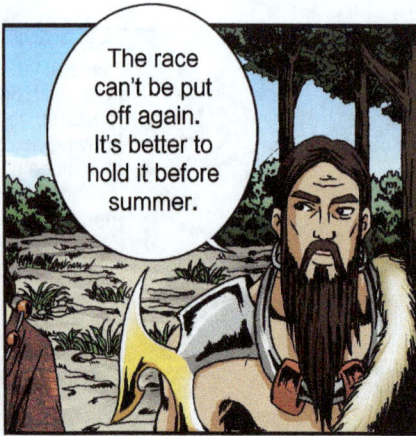

The race can't be put off again. It's better to hold it before summer.

Isn't that too hasty?

The horse racing is held to select the king of the Ling Tribe. If he can't adapt to this change, how can he be the king of our tribe? Ahchoo!

Bah! Stop talking about the adaptability. You got a cold several years ago, but you still have not got over it!

We have been here several years. Now, the people lead a stable life. It is time to select our chieftain.

Right, right! The golden seat and Cholmo should see their owner!

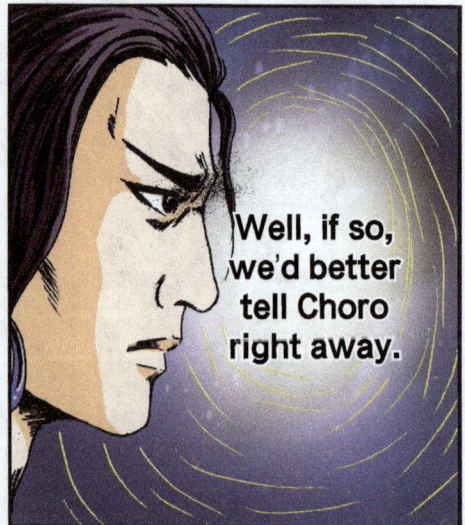

Well, if so, we'd better tell Choro right away.

Alas, the golden seat and jewelry can be easily arranged, but Cholmo...

I asked her to find Choro on the condition that she wouldn't be the prize of the race.

Chalho, you see...

Take it easy, everybody. I have reached agreement with Cholmo about that already.

Great! Only the Ling King deserves Cholmo.

Choro doesn't deserve her.

If she is unwilling to be the queen, don't force her.

It is an extraodinary honor for her to be the queen. Which girl in the tribe doesn't want to be?

In the large tent of Chalho

I don't want to be the queen.

Clatter!

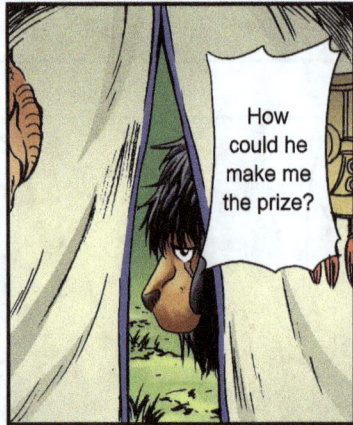

How could he make me the prize?

Doggie, let's go. I can stay no longer in this house.

Bow-wow!

My father is so unreasonable!

On the path in the mountain forest...

How could they break their promise?

I went a long way to find Choro, but it was all for nothing.

Buddha, bless me! Send one to lift me out of the misery.

Yu!

Cholmo,

where are you going?

Is he really coming?

A deity? No, a monster!

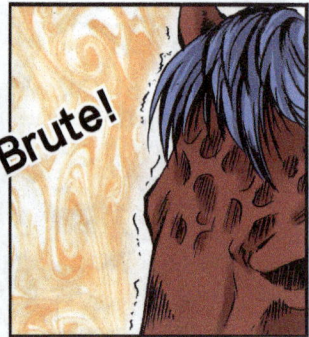

You little bastard!

Clattering—

Pa!

Let go!

Do you think you can get everything just with a smart horse?

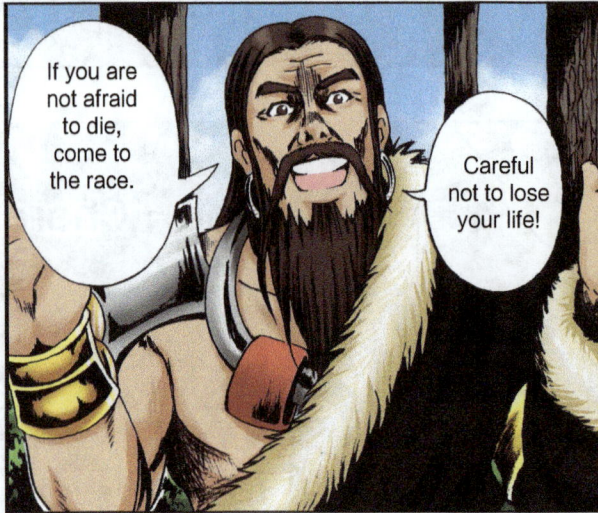

If you are not afraid to die, come to the race.

Careful not to lose your life!

Rest assured. I will surely come.

Humph! You pup, prepare to meet your doom!

Cholmo?

I...

I thought you were different from them.

Didn't expect...

You are no better!

Why do the men depend on their horses instead of themselves if they want to be the chieftain?

Why should a girl be the prize? How can you decide her fate so easily?

Why...

Boohoo...

Come with me!

Our homeland.

How beautiful!

As long as I can become the king of the Ling Tribe, I will do everything.

When I was driven out, I lost it... I was heartbroken. This time, I will own and protect it!

I must become the king of the Ling Tribe!

You can do it!

If you want to help...

You can prepare saddle and stirrup for me!

You...

Wanna go back?

No, it is really beautiful here.

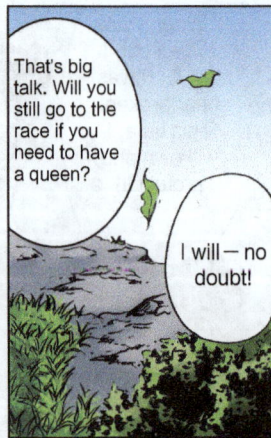

That's big talk. Will you still go to the race if you need to have a queen?

I will — no doubt!

...

Several days later

Horse race is held...

Prepared for the New King!

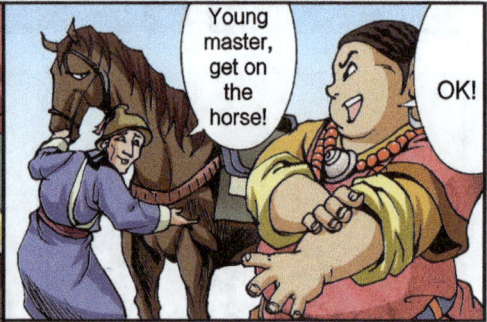

Ah!

Young master!

Haha...

Who dares to make fun of me? After my father wins the championship,

I will be the prince of the Ling Tribe!

So noisy...

I wonder what is keeping Choro.

How handsome Chatsa is!

Chatsa!

I like Zhaotoin!

Bad taste!

Choro...

Why aren't you here?

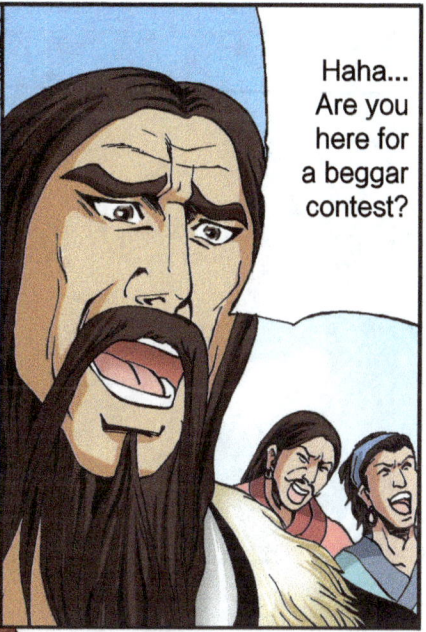

Haha... Are you here for a beggar contest?

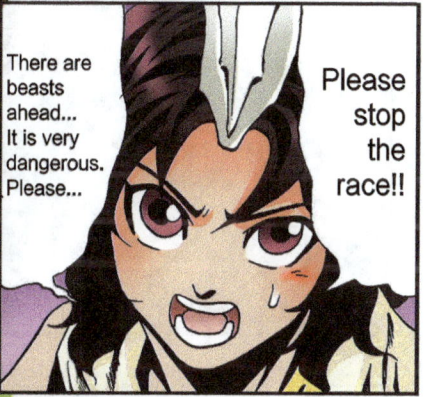

There are beasts ahead... It is very dangerous. Please...

Please stop the race!!

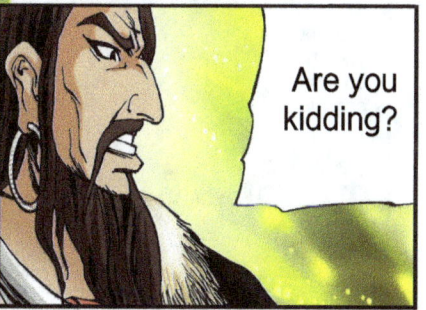

Are you kidding?

Hiss——

071

These are the elites of my tribe!

Which of them fears beasts?!

These beasts are not ordinary ones. They are savage... No, they are monsters!

Get lost if you are afraid. Don't bullshit!

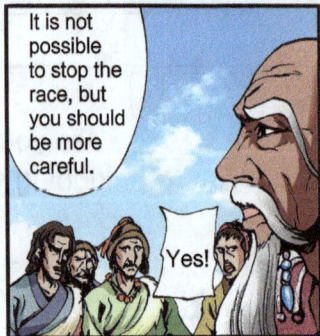

It is not possible to stop the race, but you should be more careful.

Yes!

Sissy!

Then, warriors, for the future of our Ling Tribe...

Why...

Choro...
Alas!

Let's go
to Gori
Mountain!

Go to the
finishing
line to
wait for
them.

Let's go
to the
finishing
line.

Okay...

...

I saw monsters here just now.

Ta...ta...

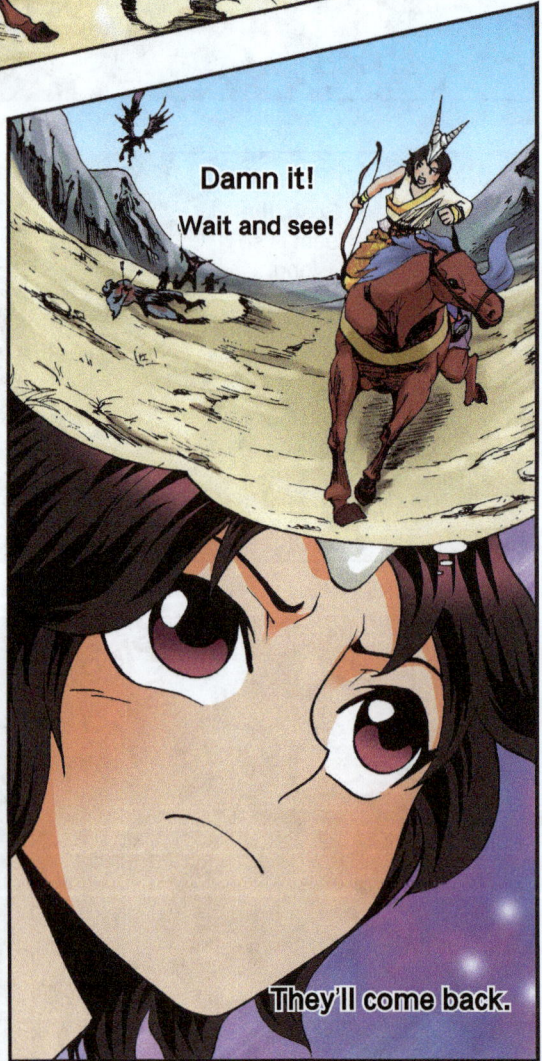

Damn it!
Wait and see!

They'll come back.

I remember the snare is nearby.

Found it!

Cha!

Hong——

What happened?

Ah? A trap?!

Ambush! Be careful!

Whiz!

Whiz!

Humph! I'm leaving now.

There are really beasts here.

No! Not beasts... They are...

Monsters!

Don't let any of them pass!

Attack them all!

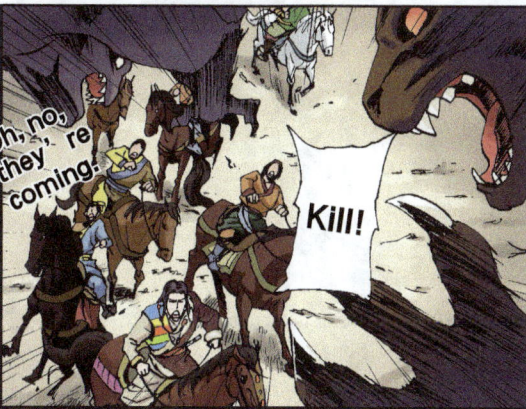

Oh, no, they're coming!

Kill!

Damn it! None of us took weapons to the race.

Roaring!

Ping!!

Bang!

What terrible monsters, Damn!

Oh —

Chapter 10

Becoming King at the Horse Race

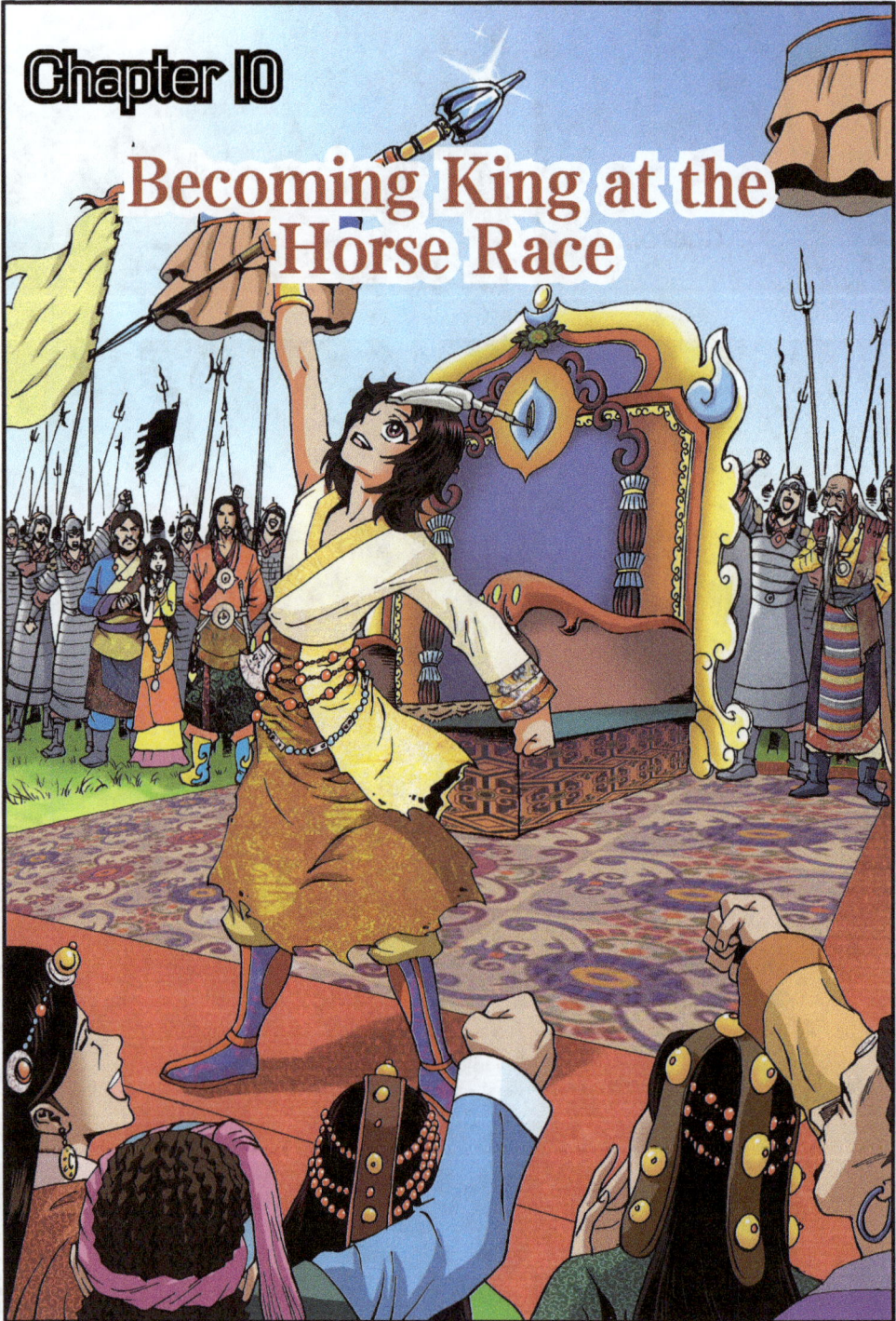

Ah!

Cho... Choro?

No matter where you monsters come from, you can not harm the brothers of my tribe!!

On the hillside at the finishing line...

Someone is coming!

• • •

Coming, coming...

Who will it be?

Ta—

Father... I'm sorry.

I would rather die than wed this sort of person!

Ta...

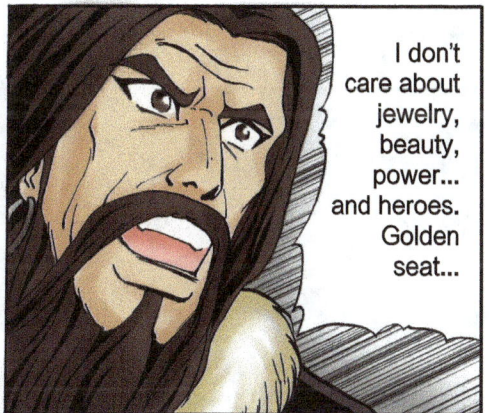

I don't care about jewelry, beauty, power... and heroes. Golden seat...

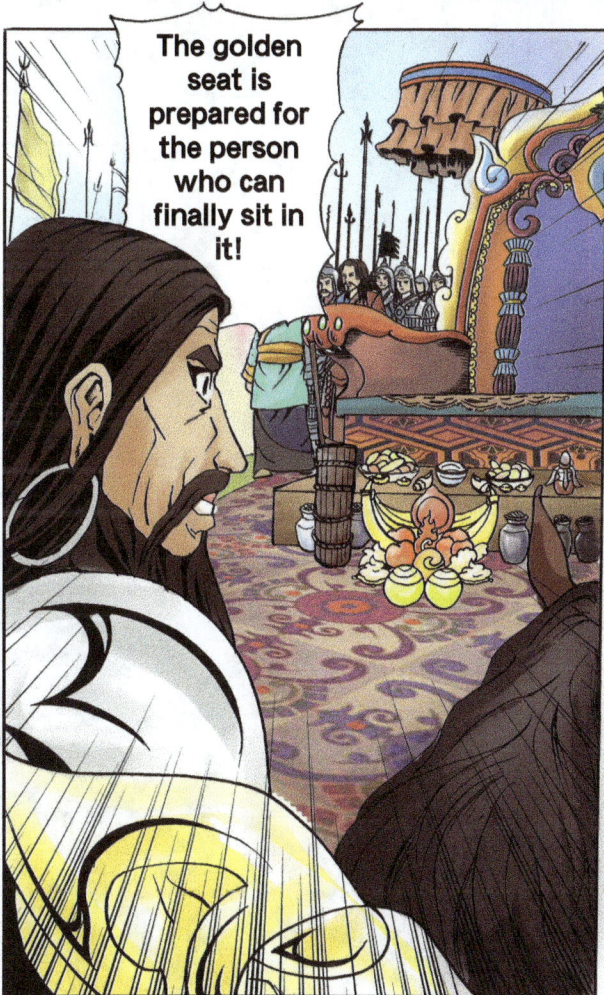

The golden seat is prepared for the person who can finally sit in it!

Whirr——

Whirr!

Whirr!

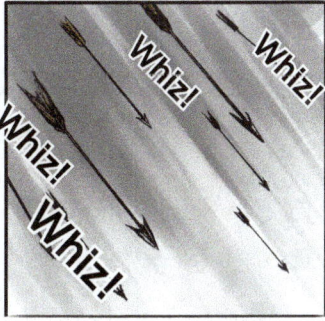

097

What...

What happened?

The golden seat doesn't belong to you!!

Cangpa Wolo (one of the three most handsome men of the Ling Tribe)

The golden seat only belongs to the person who is willing to sacrifice himself for the brothers of his tribe!

Kunshitibo (fortuneteller of the Ling Tribe)

And the person who can defeat the monsters with his divine power!

Gunkar Nyima (Great doctor of the Ling Tribe)

And the person who refuses treatment and wins the championship on his own!

Who are they referring to?

...

Yes!

Golden seat

Unfair!

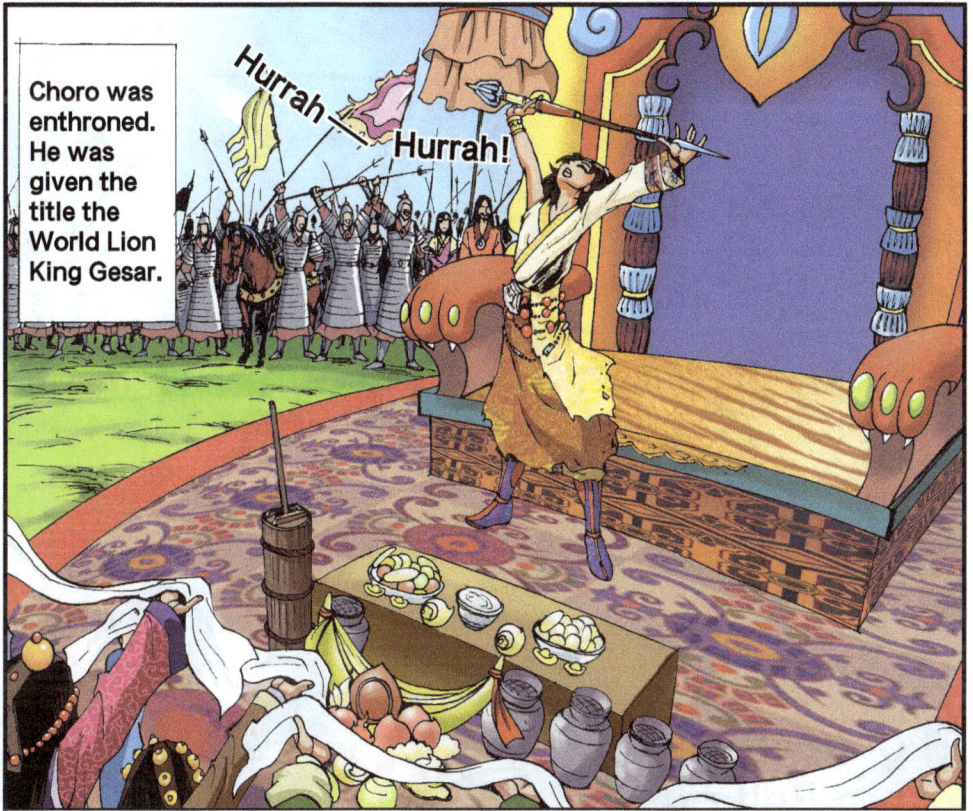

Choro was enthroned. He was given the title the World Lion King Gesar.

Hurrah

Hurrah!

Your Majesty, try on this gown!

Congratulations, Your Majesty! Try on this tunic!

Your Majesty...

Your Majesty...

Bronze Armor

Victorious
White Helmet

Immortal
Longevity
Underwear

Longevity–
knot Belt of
the Warrior

Megatron
Dragon's
Boots

Yarkang Demon State in the Cairan Morbo Plain in the north.

You three...

Even had the nerve to come back.

Sorry...

Calm down, Your Majesty, Though we couldn't prevent them from selecting the king...

Cha!

We...have captured a special man.

To be continued...

Coming Up Next

As Gesar's journey continues, divine interventions and spiritual teachings guide his path. Discover how celestial beings shape his destiny and prepare him for future battles.**

How will these mystical encounters influence his path? Continue to Volume 2 to delve deeper into Gesar's spiritual enlightenment and his preparations for future battles.*